"Damages are a critically important component of complex commercial litigation, but at times the damages case gets lost in the liability issues. In the Pragmatic Solution, Rick Bero draws from his extensive experience as a testifying expert witness to clearly and concisely guide litigators in building a pragmatic damages case from start to finish. As Rick says, he's providing a blueprint to building a damages castle. The Pragmatic Solution teaches us, as litigators, how to keep the damages case in sight and weave it with the liability case. Any commercial litigator, from new associate to senior partner, would benefit from Rick's advice on constructing a practical and successful damages case."

—Experienced Commercial Litigation Partner
at Am Law 200 Firm

"*The Litigator's Damages Blueprint: The Pragmatic Solution* provides an accessible framework for approaching the damages analysis in the most complex cases. Rick Bero's practical approach will help even the most seasoned litigators maximize their client's recovery. A must read for litigators."

—Experienced Patent Litigation Partner
from 1000+-Person Law Firm

The Litigator's Damages Blueprint:

The Pragmatic Solution

Richard F. Bero

The Litigator's Damages Blueprint: The Pragmatic Solution

422 Doty, LLC
N16 W23217 Stone Ridge Drive, Suite 150
Waukesha, WI 53188

Limit of Liability/Disclaimer of Warranty:

Throughout the book, I discuss real world case examples. The intent of these examples is to provide color to the concepts discussed based on my own experience working with my team and various litigators. Each case example is based on actual cases I have worked on. They are also based upon my current recollections and interpretations of events and circumstances in each case. Undoubtedly, I have mis-remembered facts and circumstances in some of the cases. And, in some instances, I have also modified facts or figures. No warranty may be created or extended by sales representatives or written sales materials. Neither the publisher nor author shall be liable for any loss of profit or any other commercial damages, including but not limited to special, incidental, consequential, or other damages.

Publishing and editorial team:
Author Bridge Media, www.AuthorBridgeMedia.com
Project Manager and Editorial Director: Helen Chang
Publishing Manager: Laurie Aranda
Cover Design: Mark Gelotte

Library of Congress Control Number: 2019913433

ISBN: 978-1-7332923-0-6 – paperback
978-1-7332923-1-3 – hardcover
978-1-7332923-2-0 – ebook

Ordering Information:

Quantity sales. Special discounts are available on quantity purchases by corporations, associations, and others. For details, contact the publisher at the address above.

Printed in United States of America.

DEDICATION

I dedicate this book to my grandfather Arthur Julius Bero. Grandpa exuded calm, love, dedication, stoicism, and pragmatism. Though he passed many years ago, he continues to live quietly in my thoughts and my heart.

THANKS

There are so many people to thank. First, I thank my team at The BERO Group, particularly my assistant, Beth Bergman, for coordinating and putting up with me throughout the process, and Joe Laur, a director who has been with me step-by-step on many of my cases for the last nineteen years.

I also send out a huge thanks to Joan Eads. We first "met" when Joan was cross-examining me at trial. She subsequently hired me as an expert on multiple cases. After retiring from her legal practice, Joan joined our team and provided enthusiasm and invaluable guidance for eight years. Joan has since retired, but she nonetheless provided insights and edits on this book. She has been and continues to be an inspiration.

Next, I thank the many litigators who reviewed drafts, provided comments on, and encouraged the development of this book. You all know who you are. And thanks to Todd Goldberg of NorthStar Lit Technologies, a trial exhibit expert and consultant extraordinaire, for his insights and unending humor. I would also like to thank my friends at Strategic Coach for inspiring and encouraging me to write this book, especially Kayanne Ratay, my program advisor. Finally, I would like to thank the team at Author Bridge Media for patiently walking me through the book-writing process.

CONTENTS

INTRODUCTION

It always seems impossible until it is done.

— Nelson Mandela

The Litigation Battlefield

Litigation is a battle.

It takes place on a verbal and written battlefield that continually changes right up to and throughout trial. Commercial litigators juggle a never-ending list of variables, demands, and priorities. With so many issues to prioritize, you can easily neglect important components until the case schedule demands that you pay attention.

Damages can be one of those important components that fall below the radar.

Coordinating damages issues comes with its own set of significant challenges: court deadlines, client expectations, and litigation costs, among others. You are managing uncertainty, risks, and moving parts, perhaps without extensive experience developing damages issues.

As a commercial litigator, you have likely already worked on or will work on cases involving damages. But even if you have, perhaps your damages cases have not made it to trial, or at least not recently. Some financial concepts or terminology underlying damages might be foreign to you. Certain elements could be foggy. Confronting these obstacles while dealing with the roller coaster of the litigation process increases the likelihood of missed opportunities, gaps in the damages analysis, or a disconnect between liability and damages.

Whether representing plaintiffs or defendants, without the right preparation and coordination, you may miss damages opportunities or put your damages case at risk, leaving you weak and wounded on the litigation battlefield.

Hochosterwitz Castle

Built into a dolomite rock mountain two thousand feet above sea level, the Hochosterwitz Castle in Austria has stood the tests of battle and time. With clear skies, you can see the striking white-and-gray castle from twenty miles away. Through the eleventh and twelfth centuries, the castle served as a refuge for locals from multiple punishing attacks by Turkish forces.

A popular legend holds that Countess Margaret of Tyrol sent troops to attack Hochosterwitz in retaliation for being denied her inheritance after her father died in 1335. The soldiers inside the castle decided to bluff: they slaughtered their only ox, stuffed it with corn, and catapulted it over the castle walls. It was meant to send a message that they were so well supplied, they could use food as a weapon. It worked, and Countess Margaret's men withdrew.

After the castle had survived the onslaught of the Turks and the Countess, in 1571 a new owner hired a renowned military architect to fortify the castle with an armory and the unusual addition of fourteen gates.

These gates, staggered along the long, uphill path to the castle, created an impenetrable defense system. As would-be attackers attempted to breach each gate, they would come under attack from multiple vantage points around the castle. It is said that no one ever made it past the fourth gate.

With its mountaintop location, rock-solid construction, ingenious gate system, and defense by cunning soldiers, Hochosterwitz Castle was never conquered. It sits peacefully now as a tourist attraction, a reminder of more tumultuous times.[1]

Figure 1: Image courtesy of Felix Mittermeier from Pixabay

---

1 For more information on Hochosterwitz Castle, see Wikipedia and https://www.burg-hochosterwitz.com/en/.

Build Your Damages Castle

Like castles, the best damages cases are designed and built to withstand attacks.

This book will teach you the steps to build your "Damages Castle." Whether you are representing a plaintiff or defendant, this process gives you the tools to build a castle with a logical blueprint, strong foundation, and sturdy walls. Large or small, your castle will be built to withstand a siege.

This is not a how-to-calculate-damages book. Rather, this book will provide you with a process that our team calls "The Pragmatic Solution" to help you manage your damages case. It offers a structure to engage fully with your damages analysis as you move from early preparation up to and through trial. It guides you to work with your damages expert to develop a well-reasoned analysis that will align with your liability case.

The Pragmatic Solution answers such crucial questions as: *When do I start thinking about damages? What should I be anticipating next? How will this play out at trial? How do I build the strongest damages case?*

You can begin to use this process as you take on your next case, and you can follow it all the way through to the conclusion of trial. Using these steps, you will be positioned to create a pragmatic damages analysis.

The Reasoning

You may wonder why a damages expert would want to write a book for litigators. Why would a damages expert write *anything* down, for that matter, knowing he could be cross-examined on everything? It's a question I have been asked many times by the attorneys I spoke with as I wrote this book.

The answer is simple. I hope The Pragmatic Solution will help others who haven't spent their careers in this field.

The hugely positive response and enthusiasm this book has received from experienced litigators confirmed my desire to get The Pragmatic Solution out into the world.

Pragmatic History

My team and I know The Pragmatic Solution works because we've used it successfully for many years.

I cofounded The BERO Group's predecessor in 1995 in Milwaukee, Wisconsin, after working at both a large international consulting firm and a Big Eight (now Big Four) accounting firm. Our company provides financial and accounting consulting services and expert testimony pertaining to financial damages, valuation, and fraud.

Based in Wisconsin, we are Green Bay Packers fans (at least most of us are). Yes, some people may call us "cheeseheads." My father grew up in Green Bay, and both of his parents lived there for their entire lives.

My grandfather, Arthur Julius Bero, owned a shoe repair shop on Doty Street. With the exception of his time spent as a cook in France during World War I, he rarely left Green Bay. He ran the shop six-and-a-half days a week, every week, until shortly before he passed in 1976.

My grandpa was a quiet and pragmatic man, dedicated and hardworking. He missed only one Packers home game from the team's inception until his death (and that was a preseason game). His brother played on the original 1919

Packers team with Curly Lambeau. My grandpa was my hero. His work ethic, character, and pragmatism continue to inspire me to this day.

This picture of my grandpa's shop hangs in my firm's reception area.

Iron Sharpens Iron

As iron sharpens iron, so one person sharpens another.
— Proverbs 27:17

Since I entered this field more than thirty years ago, I have been fortunate to have testified as a damages expert in approximately forty trials and one hundred depositions, as well as arbitrations and hearings across the United States.

I have served as a consultant and expert on a vast number of additional cases that did not require my testimony.

My team and I have had the opportunity to work with—and against—many outstanding litigators. In many instances, juries have awarded damages entirely consistent or mostly aligned with my testimony and analyses. In some instances, it went the other way. I have also experienced cases where I've been excluded from testifying and cases where the opposing experts have been excluded from testifying.

Throughout these cases and those of the other experts at my firm, we have learned a tremendous amount.

I have written about patent infringement damages and trade secrets damages in *The Comprehensive Guide to Economic Damages* (now in its fifth edition). I have taught as the lead instructor of intellectual property damages for the National Association of Certified Valuation Analysts for many years.

All of this is to say that I believe The Pragmatic Solution works, and it can work for you, too. Gaining a clearer focus on building your damages case alongside your liability case will position you—and your clients—for increased confidence in the integrity of your damages case.

Take It from the Pros

Every case is unique and has many different variables. It's difficult—if not impossible—to take the steps used in one case and apply them directly to another. But one thing that can be applied from one case to another is a process for building your damages case.

This book won't take long to read. You can read it in one sitting, and then come back to specific chapters as you work through the damages issues on your next case. In the time it takes to catch up on email, you'll come to understand a process for pragmatically approaching damages in your cases.

Maybe you are a highly experienced commercial litigator who fully understands damages, and you're ready to delegate the damages portions of your cases to a less-experienced litigator. You would like a consistent process and assurance the damages analysis will come together in an effective and practical manner. You want it to withstand attacks.

I am not an attorney, and I have no intention of advising you on how to do your job. Instead, I hope you will find that The Pragmatic Solution will guide you through the general concepts of a damages case. It's not specific to one type of damages. It's also not necessarily only applicable to the damages case; it may also apply to the technical-expert or industry-expert issues you and your team face.

Although I named it, and our team uses it, The Pragmatic Solution isn't entirely mine. It evolved out of observations, communications, and actions experienced in hundreds of commercial litigation matters spanning more than thirty years. It is derived from working with—and against—many incredible litigators. You are the pros. And it comes from my spectacular team, which is also made up of pros.

Let's use that combined experience to help you prepare for your next battle.

The Process

Each chapter of *The Litigator's Damages Blueprint* covers a different phase. From developing a blueprint to using an expert to your full advantage at trial, these phases provide the guidance to navigate the damages aspect of your case and develop a structured, well-reasoned plan. Some phases will overlap as you work through the very fluid damages process.

Under tight timelines, the phases may take place at the same time. For your sake, we hope not. But in commercial litigation, we relish those challenges, don't we?

Just as in building a castle, we want to start with a plan and work from the ground up. From blueprint to finished fortress, The Pragmatic Solution has five steps for building your Damages Castle.

1. **The Blueprint.** You begin with an organized and structured process. The Blueprint has two primary parts. Part one is contacting your Architect—your damages expert—early. Part two is assigning a Damages Sentry to coordinate the process. Together, these two elements provide the structure to develop your Blueprint.

2. **The Foundation.** To build the Foundation for a practical, well-supported damages case, you align

your liability and damages. By coordinating with your damages expert, you create the solid base upon which to build your Damages Castle.

3. **The Walls.** On top of the Foundation, you build your Walls. This phase typically represents the most extensive part of the damages analysis. You and your team obtain the available building materials for the Damages Castle. You continually monitor the alignment between the liability and damages and communicate frequently with your damages expert. With the Walls built properly and in the correct place, you increase the clarity and confidence in your damages analysis.

4. **The Keeps.** The Keeps are the strongest, most secure part of a castle. Here, you focus on your strengths. Your damages analysis may be complex, the terminology and data extensive and detailed. The Keeps phase prompts you to uncover and embrace the basic components upon which the damages case rests.

5. **The Castle.** Your hard work and steady communication through the first phases guide you toward your completed Castle. You understand the damages analysis and its Keeps. Your liability and damages cases are linked. You have a supportable damages analysis with solid Keeps that are entered into evidence. Now, you are ready to present a clear, compelling damages case at trial.

The Pragmatic Solution is based on the process my team and I use as we develop and work through our damages analyses. The process cannot and will not guarantee you will win your damages case. That can be a subjective determination. It also depends on variables beyond the scope of this book.

This book provides a guide for a pragmatic damages case. The process we describe helps our team. I hope it will help you and your team successfully navigate damages cases as well.

Let's get started building your Damages Castle with The Pragmatic Solution.

Chapter 1

The Blueprint—Part 1: Hire Your Architect

Blueprint, noun: *an early plan or design that explains how something might be achieved.*

— Cambridge Dictionary

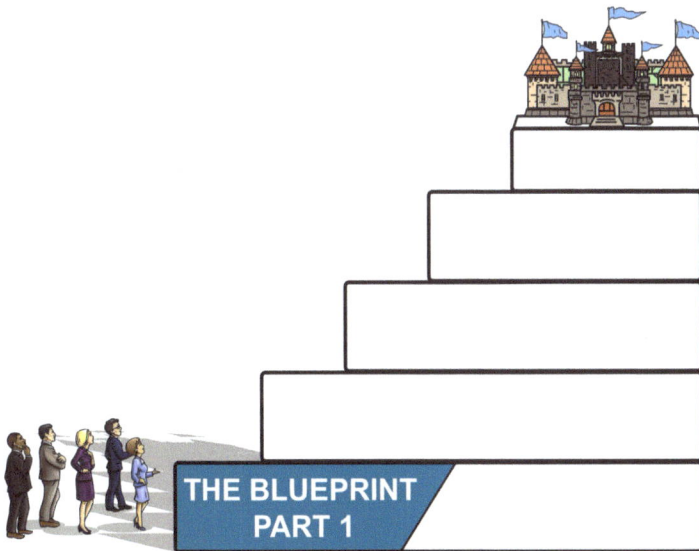

Your Focus Is Liability

This book is about damages—in other words, it's about the numbers. My team and I have seen the look in litigators' eyes when we start talking markets, sales, costs, and profits. Numbers are not often a litigator's favorite part of the case. Most litigators we have worked with do not have backgrounds in accounting, finance, or economics. It's fair to say that most would have preferred to focus on the liability and legal arguments.

You, too, may be most interested in and focused on winning the legal aspects of your case. When you get a new case, you coordinate with your client, deal with the opposing attorneys, and zero in on the liability battlefield. At this point, you don't yet have all the facts sorted out.

How and where do damages fit in? You may have dealt with damages in cases many times before. Or, possibly, not at all. Whatever your experience, if the case before you involves damages considerations, they may be significant. They may be critical. You and your team will benefit from a structured process for the damages portion of the case.

Your Architect Is Your Resource

To build a Damages Castle, you have to answer a number of questions: *Where will I build it? What kind of castle will it be? Which direction will it face? How big will it be?*

Admittedly, I have not built a medieval castle. However,

I imagine that in building a castle, one would likely hire an architect. To build your damages analysis in commercial litigation, you hire a damages expert as your Architect. For any building project—castle or commercial damages case—it makes sense to involve your architect in the planning stages.

In Real Life…Ideally, Your Architect Is an Expert

It may seem obvious to hire a damages Architect who is an expert on the issues at hand. But we have seen examples where that has not happened. In one case, within the first ten or fifteen minutes of the expert's deposition, the expert stated he was not an expert in the type of damages in his report. He also stated he was not an expert in damages. Quick deposition. The case settled a few days after this deposition.

The Initial Scope

Hiring an Architect to work on the Blueprint puts you in a position to address the initial damages scope. You want your damages expert to provide opinions on damages, but what is the scope of those opinions? If you're representing a defendant, do you want your expert to quantify a damages amount? Or do you want your expert to only opine on the shortcomings underlying the plaintiff's damages analysis?

You might narrow the scope of your expert's opinion by

asking them to make certain assumptions. Some assumptions may be in dispute, and others not. If you ask your expert to make certain assumptions that are in dispute, are they critical to the analysis and otherwise supportable? Where will that support come from? Will it require another type of expert?

Of course, litigation can be unpredictable. It's difficult to know the hurdles you will face. Often you cannot predict either the cooperation the other side will provide throughout discovery or the availability of client data. How many iterations of detailed financial spreadsheets will both sides produce, and will those spreadsheets be consistent with other financial data?

Take advantage of your damages expert's knowledge in the discovery process. What are the relevant damages documents? What damages interrogatory questions could be asked? What damages questions are important for the client's potential fact witnesses? Who are the likely client personnel with damages-related knowledge? What are the key damages deposition questions for the other side's witnesses? Or for third-party witnesses?

Often, we are asked to provide input into these discovery issues, particularly by litigators we have worked with before. In other instances, discovery largely takes place without our input. Litigators who have worked with us or other experienced damages experts recognize the benefit of their damages expert's input in establishing the Blueprint of the damages case.

Start Early

Considering damages early in the litigation process helps you assess the potential damages amount your client may obtain (if you are the plaintiff) or potential damages exposure (if you are the defendant). Some cases may be relatively clear on the liability issues, and the dispute is primarily about damages. Many cases are not as clear. Regardless, addressing and uncovering the key damages considerations and parameters early on should assist you as the case progresses.

For example, early consultation with a damages expert may help guide you and your client through potential settlement. We have been involved in many of these early discussions and preliminary analyses. It may also enhance your communication with your client and help clarify their expectations.

Whether your client is a plaintiff or defendant, involving your damages expert early can quickly guide you to the key damages elements in your case. Your expert can uncover facts or unanswered questions that support—or undermine—your anticipated damages case. Regardless, your expert will raise questions that will help guide you and your client through discovery.

Each case is different and has its own intricacies specific to the industry, product, contract, or technology. There may be particular quirks to understand about the client or their relationships. There could be terminology or acronyms that nobody understands outside the accounting department, company, or industry. These intricacies and particulars take some time to digest, sort through, and connect. Give yourself and your expert enough time to process the information.

What's the Risk in Early?

While you may recognize the value in contacting your damages expert early, your client may not. Perhaps your client is reluctant to invest in an expert until it's necessary. That's understandable and quite common; we've heard these statements many times:

- *Who wants to invest now?*
- *The case likely won't go to trial.*
- *Everyone knows it will settle, right?*

Maybe everyone is sure the case won't make it to the damages phase, so the client has no desire to invest in a Damages Blueprint.

Think again of building your castle. The Blueprint, though critically important, requires little investment relative to the total castle investment. In the same way, involving a damages expert in the initial planning represents a minimal relative risk and investment. But that early intervention by an expert could make the difference between a strong and well-reasoned damages case and one that cracks or crumbles.

If you are representing a defendant, do you really want

to wait until you get the plaintiff's damages expert report before hiring your own damages expert? How informed will you be on the potential damages issues if you wait?

If you are representing a plaintiff, can you afford to wait until you're approaching next month's damages report deadline before reaching out to an expert? Are you confident you'll be able to obtain the necessary evidence to support a solid damages analysis?

There is also the practical consideration of getting the expert you want. You may have a preferred expert for a particular case, but the client wants to wait. When the time comes to contact the expert, you realize the expert has already been hired by the other side. It could also be that given late notice, your preferred expert has a scheduling conflict. We have seen this many times over the years.

In one instance, an attorney representing the plaintiff in a case sent us documents and information with a request to comment and discuss. When we received the information, I was a bit confused. The attorney apparently had wanted to hire my firm and me, when in fact, we had already been hired by the defendants.

Many of the successful litigators I have worked with over the years would also tell you to contact a damages expert early.

When damages are likely to play a potentially significant role in a case, it is certainly beneficial to gain an initial understanding of the probable damages issues, obstacles, and challenges.

In Real Life . . . When Early Doesn't Happen

A few years ago, on a midsummer Monday, my phone rang. A litigator asked if we could help on an industrial patent case. Client was the defendant. Time was tight. How tight? The report was due the following Friday—eleven days away. And the case protective order required a seven-day waiting period. In other words, we would not be able to see the plaintiff's damages expert report until the following Monday, just a few days before my report was due.

The litigator team had just taken over the case from another firm. They were learning with us. The circumstances were less than ideal for a thoroughly thought-out Blueprint and Foundation. Considering the time constraints, our analysis and damages report were solid. Nonetheless, the Walls, while strong, undoubtedly could have been planned, investigated, and analyzed more thoroughly with additional time.

In Real Life . . . When Early Happens

A few years ago, I was brought in on a commercial litigation matter involving a defective product in the transportation industry. The timing was relatively early, many months before initial damages expert reports were due. Our client was the plaintiff. The company was struggling to manage defective components provided by a significant supplier. At the time, my client believed damages were likely in the low seven-figure range.

We asked questions early in the case that, with the benefit of time, led to extensive and coordinated discovery with the plaintiff's customers. That discovery led to an understanding the damages were well into the eight-figure range—multiples of what the client first anticipated.

How Early Is Early?

What does contacting the damages expert early look like? Is early relative to the date the complaint was filed, or the date discovery closes, or the date the damages reports are due, or the trial date? It depends on the potential importance and significance of the damages.

Occasionally, early is before a case is even filed. Inevitably, the initial investment in time and fees is relatively minimal. In return, the attorneys obtain potentially valuable damages information and perspective on hurdles, obstacles, and opportunities.

In some instances, early damages assessments guide the direction of your entire case. In the transportation case discussed earlier, this led to the discovery of information that demonstrated a larger-than-anticipated damages amount. Had the facts been different, they may have led to an early recognition that damages were a smaller amount, or no amount at all.

The potential high reward of consulting early outweighs

the relatively small investment risk. At a minimum, you now have your damages expert in place with a signed engagement letter.

In some instances, we have been hired by a potential plaintiff to prepare preliminary analyses before the decision has been made to file a complaint. In other instances, a defendant has hired our team shortly after a complaint was filed to provide preliminary assessments of potential damages.

In some cases, early may be later. Perhaps initial legal wrangling and preliminary legal issues need to be sorted out before the damages discovery begins to take place. Perhaps a slow legal process may unfold wherein the parties agree to put off damages until later. In these instances, early may be relative to the damages report dates.

Get the Castle You Envision

You would hire an architect to draw up your castle blueprints. In developing the plans and scope of your damages case, wouldn't you want to hire and get input from your Damages Architect? It could be the difference between building a Hochosterwitz Castle and a house of sticks.

Getting the Damages Castle you want involves collaboration and communication with your Architect. Even when you're busy and pulled in many directions, you will still want to maintain some level of communication with your damages expert. That's where the Damages Sentry comes in. In the next chapter, we'll look at the key role of the Damages Sentry in ensuring that you build the strongest case.

Chapter 2

The Blueprint—Part 2:
Your Damages Sentry

Sentry, noun: *a soldier standing guard at a point of passage (such as a gate).*

— Merriam-Webster

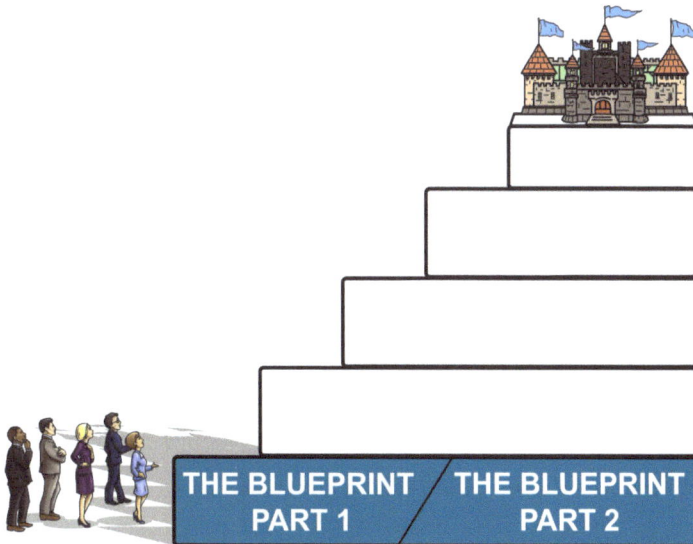

Three Approaches

At this point, it's still early in the case, and you have your Architect in place. How do you create an effective working relationship with your Architect that lasts from the initial stages until the end of the case?

You recognize that your damages expert is different from you and your fellow litigation team members: he or she is independent, not an advocate. At the same time, you cooperate, work, and communicate with your damages expert through the development and presentation of your damages case.

Litigators generally take one of three approaches when hiring and working with a damages expert. The first approach is to hire an expert to provide a somewhat predetermined damages analysis. If you are representing a plaintiff, this approach likely leads you toward an expert prepared to present the biggest possible number, regardless of support or foundation. If you are representing a defendant, this approach leads you toward an expert prepared to present zero or minimal damages, again regardless of support or foundation.

Without the proper support and analysis, this could be described as hiring a mercenary. With this approach, the attorney does not receive pragmatic guidance from the expert. The Damages Castle is prone to be weak and may not stand up to the litigation battle.

This approach is not consistent with The Pragmatic

Solution. While my firm does not employ this approach, we have seen it and understand there may be strategic, cost, or other reasons behind it. In some cases, the mercenary approach may be chosen inadvertently.

The second approach involves hiring the damages expert to take care of the damages for you. The damages expert deals with the numbers, while you focus on what you enjoy—the liability and legal arguments. This approach can seem efficient, but it has a potential drawback. I call this the blinders approach, because it may keep your expert in the dark about key elements of the case.

Even if you start out fully engaged with your expert, other aspects of the case eventually demand your attention, and it can be tempting to leave the expert alone. You may think, *This is what I hired my damages expert to do—it's their responsibility.* This passivity can effectively put blinders on the expert, compromising their ability to create the best damages analysis.

The third—and best—approach is The Pragmatic Solution approach. Here, you look to your expert, your Architect, as a resource. At the same time, however, you recognize the expert is different from your fellow attorneys. While you are an advocate, your expert is independent and objective.

Your damages expert has likely written many reports, read countless opposing expert reports, and participated in numerous trials and depositions. They should understand the importance of their independence. Get the most from their experience by involving them in identifying and obtaining relevant damages evidence. Use their objective, independent eyes and work closely with them to coordinate the liability and damages cases.

Your expert can be the Architect for your Blueprint and your entire damages case. How do you make use of your resource most effectively?

Damages Sentry

You likely have other members on your litigation team. All of you are teammates, or fellow soldiers, and one of you is the leader. How do you maximize the value of your damages expert? A simple yet powerful approach is to designate yourself or one of your litigator teammates as the primary liaison with your expert: the Damages Sentry.

In writing this book, I have thought back to many of the trials I have attended and testimony I have given over the years. I have also discussed concepts underlying The Pragmatic Solution with litigators and heard their experiences with other damages experts. If there is one point that stands out, it is the value of a Damages Sentry.

Assign your Damages Sentry—perhaps you—as the primary communicator between your litigation team, your damages expert, and the client.

The Damages Sentry's most important role is working directly and closely with the expert and the expert's team to keep communication channels open. The Damages Sentry is the gatekeeper of information, maintaining the flow of relevant information to and from and among the litigation team, your client, the damages expert's team, and other experts or witnesses. In this manner, the Damages Sentry coordinates and learns about the damages analyses.

Make it clear what communication method works best for all parties. For many of us, email is the preferred communication mode. For others, it may be in-person meetings or phone calls.

Castle Location and Materials

Regardless of the communication mode used, what type of information will be useful for your expert? Certainly, each case is different. At the same time, it is relatively common for litigators to underestimate the wide range of information the expert requires to build a thorough damages analysis. This information provides the potential building materials for the Damages Castle.

Your damages expert may be interested in an upcoming deposition of the other side's marketing person. Your expert may also be interested in production, purchasing, or customer depositions. By communicating about upcoming depositions, ongoing document production, and interrogatory questions and answers, you give your expert the opportunity to gather the most relevant information.

Often, my team is asked to develop a list of questions or topics for upcoming depositions of marketing, accounting, finance, customer, technical, production, and administrative personnel, among others. Other times, we unfortunately learn of depositions after the fact. *Oh, we did that dep last month. Would you like to see the transcript? We didn't talk to you about it because it was marketing, not numbers stuff.*

Sometimes these missed opportunities are due to distractions. Deadlines, briefs, motions, discovery, and a host of other obstacles interfere. The Damages Sentry can help avoid these pitfalls. Sharing information about documents, upcoming depositions, interrogatories, declarations, dates, and deadlines is crucial.

Certainly, litigation is an ever-changing scheduling and communication challenge. Sometimes, a Damages Sentry starts out focused on damages but gets pulled in other, more pressing, directions. A long communication gap follows. In other situations, multiple Damages Sentries share the job of communicating with the expert, and the process breaks down. Maybe a deposition takes place and a damages topic is missed.

In Real Life . . . Missing Damages Sentry

Remember the industrial patent case with just eleven days to prepare the damages expert report? After the expert report and my deposition, a communications gap developed as the case worked its way toward trial.

We were in a condensed time frame between expert discovery and trial. The attorneys were under enormous pressure, having taken over the case shortly before my report due date and just a few months before trial. Leading up to trial, they had more pressing concerns than communicating with their damages expert. After my deposition, there was limited communication.

We understood the trial dates were scheduled a few months after my deposition. We also understood the case was unlikely to settle. Our client was the defendant. The plaintiff's claim was well into eight figures. My team and I prepared for the trial, assuming it was going to take place.

Our challenge was keeping the damages testimony aligned with any liability developments, not knowing whether our supporting facts and data would come into evidence before my testimony. Were we describing a Castle aligned with the Foundation? Were we describing data, facts, and information the jurors would be familiar with? It turned out there were some gaps.

I testified to the defendant's relatively low accused sales and profits to frame the plaintiff's damages claim as being far in excess of the defendant's sales of the accused products. Prior to my testimony, the jurors had not heard the defendant's comparatively low sales amounts because the defendant's company witnesses had not talked about them. The trial exhibits had not shown the defendant's low sales or profit amounts either. My testimony was the first time the jury had seen or heard of those relatively low amounts.

What were the jurors thinking? After seeing and hearing all of the prior witnesses and testimony and trial exhibits, without reference to those relatively low amounts, perhaps the jurors wondered, *If these amounts were really so low, why haven't we heard about them before now? Why are we now hearing about them from this witness after all of these other witnesses never mentioned them?*

The verdict came in between our number and the plaintiff's number, though it was closer to the plaintiff's number. Was it because of gaps? We can't know. What we do know is there could have been better alignment between the facts and data underlying the analysis and the damages testimony. If you have been through many trials, you know this is not unusual.

In Real Life . . . Active Damages Sentry

In contrast to the example above, our Damages Sentry was active from start to finish in the following case.

The liability issues in this case involved complex technical patent claims. The relevant information was in some cases very difficult to obtain. The attorney secured documents quickly and coordinated discussions with foreign manufacturers, technical experts, and fact witnesses, among others. The attorney spent a few days working in our office to ensure we received the necessary information. To be fair, we do brew high-quality strong, dark coffee at our office.

Through his efforts and communication, the Damages Castle was firmly built in the right place to withstand the battle. Our extensive collaboration meant the attorney really knew my analysis. This translated into clear and concise trial testimony. He similarly understood the weaknesses in the opposing experts' analysis, translating into effective cross-examination. The trial was a success. The jury determined our client did not infringe.

Because of this outcome, you may be tempted to conclude the damages portion of the case was a waste of time and money. But what if liability had been found? And what effect did the damages portion of the case have on the liability case?

Our Damages Sentry was superb. We had a strong, pragmatic damages position supported by the liability case. The case was not bifurcated; both damages experts testified and were cross-examined, and fact witnesses spoke to damages issues.

Anticipate the Other Side's Castle

Ideally, the Damages Sentry is more than a communicator, coordinator, and planner. As part of the process, the Damages Sentry is ideally positioned to work with the Architect to anticipate the other side's potential damages positions.

Anticipating the other side's potential damages positions can be useful in multiple ways. It may assist in the gathering of building materials. It may guide you to obtain and produce certain data or information from your client early on in the case that helps streamline your discovery focus. Alternatively, it may lead to an early recognition that there will be extensive discovery required or that your defendant client faces a potentially large damages amount. It may provide an early reality check on your plaintiff client's potential claimed damages amount.

Anticipating the other side's Damages Castle will likely contribute to discovery, including taking depositions of opposing fact witnesses, industry or technical experts, and opposing damages experts.

Damages Sentry Qualifications and the Handoff

One consideration is the experience and qualifications of your Damages Sentry. We have worked with Damages Sentries who are senior partners with extensive damages experience. We have worked with others who are dealing with their first case involving damages and some who have never taken or defended a deposition before. Of course, the more experienced the Damages Sentry, the greater the foresight and recognition of how and where the damages analysis fits into the overall case. The reverse is also true.

In some cases, we have seen a handoff. Often, it takes place as the case moves closer to trial. Typically, a younger litigator hands off the Damages Sentry role to a more experienced litigator. This approach can work well. Ultimately, the experienced litigator works through the expert's direct testimony together with the expert, and they collaborate in preparing for the cross-examination of the opposing damages expert.

I have also seen handoffs go the other way. In one instance, the senior litigator had loosely acted as the Damages Sentry. I say loosely, because while the senior litigator knew more about my analysis than the other litigators, his understanding of it was somewhat limited. The handoff took place the night before I was scheduled to testify. The senior litigator relied on a less experienced litigator to work through the direct testimony preparation with me.

Meanwhile, the senior litigator still intended to take my direct the next day at trial. This is not an approach I would encourage. Ideally, before entering the courtroom, the litigator taking the expert's direct testimony knows the questions they will be asking the expert.

Discoverability and Protective Orders

Is communication with your expert discoverable? In my experience, it generally has not been for many years in most venues, unless the communication is something the expert relies upon. Still, is discoverability sorted out in your case? Is there an agreement between the parties? Is there a protective order your expert needs to sign and be cleared on before providing them any information? And who needs to sign the protective order? Just the expert, or the expert's entire team?

Keep Your Head Up

I am an enthusiastic (albeit novice) mountain biker. Those of you who mountain bike will know the first important guidance you are given is to look ahead—not right in front of your bike. You want to look where you're going. Looking ahead on the trail enables you to anticipate and prepare for rocks, roots, sand, trees, turns, and other obstacles.

Alternatively, if you look down right in front of your bike, you may lose your balance. You diminish your ability to anticipate. Having fallen many times, painfully and without grace, I know it's always because uncertainty and a lack of discipline took over. I looked down.

The same can be true for damages. When you hire your Architect early and assign a Damages Sentry, you begin to look ahead. You are in a position to identify key damages issues early, you are better able to anticipate and prepare to make decisions, you can dedicate resources (or not), and you can effectively chart a course toward the potential trial. You have a Blueprint.

With your Blueprint in hand, it's time to lay the Foundation for your Damages Castle.

Chapter 3

The Foundation

Foundation, noun: *an underlying base or support,* especially the whole masonry substructure of a building.

— *Merriam-Webster*

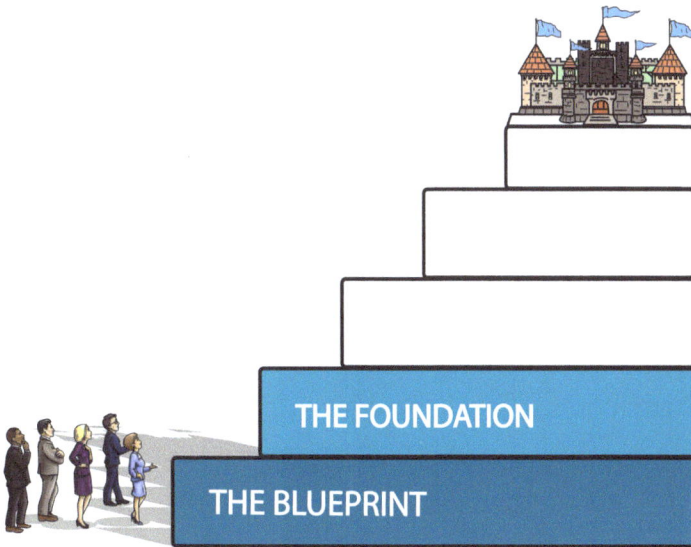

THE FOUNDATION

THE BLUEPRINT

Define the Wrongdoing

How do you begin building your solid Damages Foundation? First, refine your Blueprint: take a closer look, test it, and make sure it's right. The initial Blueprint may be perfectly fine, but you still want to ensure you're not building your Foundation in the wrong place.

Your damages analysis is usually guided by the practical definition of the alleged wrongdoing. To refine your initial Blueprint, define the wrongdoing in a practical manner. You might think, *Well, it's a contract case, so the breach of contract is the wrongdoing . . . duh.* In many cases, you're right. Defining the wrongdoing can be that straightforward.

However, you may have encountered many different types of alleged wrongdoings: patent infringement, breach of contract, tortuous interference, trademark infringement, antitrust, trade secret misappropriation, etc. Within the various types of wrongdoing categories, there may be various potential forms of damages. In other words, different wrongdoings have different consequences.

A supplier may have breached a contract by failing to supply a product to a customer. The alleged wrongdoing is a breach of that supply agreement. But what if the breach is subtler or more nuanced? What if the breach derives from the defendant providing a defective product? Or partially defective product? Or from supplying some of the products late? Or supplying them in the wrong color? The list of possibilities is endless. The type of breach or the way in which the alleged breach occurred may directly affect the damages analysis.

Patent infringement cases often warrant such a nuanced practical definition of the alleged wrongdoing. There are two primary forms of damages in utility patent cases: lost profits and/or reasonable royalties. Various facts and circumstances could lead the damages case toward one, the other, or both forms.

The alleged infringement of the various claims is often highly technical. The analyses, opinions, and testimony of your technical expert and the opposing technical expert are involved and complicated. Initially, it might seem as though the damages will naturally flow from the infringement. However, it can be difficult to assure your damages case is tied to the infringement.

Patented technology usually does not exist in a vacuum. If it's a patented feature, it probably exists in a product or products. Those products flow in and through a particular market, involving manufacturers, distributors, and customers. The patented technology may be important or not. All of these variables are part of the context.

The technology's underlying value often represents the benefit it provides in the context of the product and market in which it participates. The product and market provide context for the value of the patented technology.

In Real Life . . . Sorting Out Patents

A number of years ago, my team and I worked on behalf of a plaintiff in a patent infringement case in the financial services industry. There were numerous patents at issue, all pertaining to various devices used to scan, denominate, and sort paper currency. The patents were dense and relatively complex, encompassing, for example, optical scanning involving complex algorithms.

To a layperson, the patents all appeared to cover essentially the same basic invention. The patents had overlapping titles and specifications. While the patents all related to similar devices, they covered different capabilities or features, such as device size, counterfeit detection, and others.

Early in the case, I spent multiple days in a conference room working with the litigation team's Damages Sentry sorting out the different inventions disclosed and claimed in each patent. While this endeavor took a significant amount of time and effort, it set the foundation for aligning the liability and damages analyses.

Alignment—Damages and Liability

You have asked and answered the question, *What is the alleged wrongdoing? Your next question will help you align your damages analysis to the alleged wrongdoing. How does that alleged wrongdoing cause damages?* (Recognizing that while many forms of damages are based on the proximate cause principle, some forms, such as statutory damages, are not.)

Aligning your damages and liability means the two are linked. Your damages analysis may be dependent on a variety of variables, but it should be aligned with your liability case.

Without properly setting your foundation, your castle collapses. If you haven't aligned your Damages analysis with the alleged wrongdoing, it may be entirely irrelevant. While you may have built a beautiful castle, you set the foundation in the wrong place, or you missed the foundation altogether. Your castle was inadvertently built on an over-hanging cliff . . . on the wrong battlefield.

In Real Life . . . Footings Poured on an Over-Hanging Cliff

A number of years ago, I worked on behalf of a defendant in a patent matter in the medical device field. The plaintiff's damages expert's analysis was premised on the idea that the patented technology was quite valuable. A particular product line with the patented technology had been extremely successful relative to product lines without the patented technology. It sounded logical.

However, during the deposition of the plaintiff's chief financial officer, it became evident that this highly profitable product line did not actually include the patented technology. Rather, one of the other, less successful product lines used the technology. The expert's foundation was built on an unstable foundation. It was built on an over-hanging cliff. His analysis collapsed. The case settled shortly after that deposition.

Building a Damages Castle requires a strong foundation. Building your castle on rock provides you with a solid foundation. Building your castle on an over-hanging cliff does not. You work hard to build your liability case on a solid foundation. Your damages case is no different.

Misalignment Happens More Often Than You Think

One of the telltale signs of failing to employ The Pragmatic Solution is a litigator's lack of understanding of their own damages expert's analysis. This becomes a problem when the analysis is clearly defective, speculative, or both. And it's an even bigger issue when the damages analysis is not aligned with the liability dispute.

In Real Life . . . Not Part of the Contract

In the medical device case, misalignment quickly became clear. What if the misalignment is less obvious? After all, you are not the damages expert. More often than not, misalignment between liability and damages is less than clear.

A breach of contract trial in the ethanol industry is a case in point. The plaintiff claimed lost sales and profit damages many years into the future. The expert based the projection and analysis on a contract between the parties. Upon initial review, the plaintiff's damages expert analysis seemed reasonably straightforward. Basing projections on the contract seems reasonable, right?

Yet the analysis and details were complex and required unraveling and sorting through. It turned out the projection was based primarily on claimed lost sales and profits from activities that were not included within the contract. Misalignment.

In Real Life . . . Damages before the Breach

Sometimes, the purported alignment just doesn't seem to make sense. The explanation as to how or why the alleged wrongdoing is aligned with or caused the claimed damages may not fit. Maybe you don't really understand the analysis before you. It may take some digging to uncover the misalignment.

In one case, the plaintiff alleged the defendant breached a contract for failing to develop a certain type of software. The plaintiff's damages analysis claimed lost sales and profits. It was built on various assertions and assumptions, many of which were unclear. In sorting through those assumptions, it became clear the plaintiff was claiming its damages had begun *before* the allegedly breached contract was even signed. In other words, the Damages Castle was not built on the right foundation.

Alignment May Be Complex

The alignment between the alleged wrongdoing and the damages analysis can take shape in a variety of ways. In some cases, the alignment may be straightforward. In other cases, the alignment is more complex.

Patent cases can be particularly challenging. The initial thought process in a patent case may be: (1) There is either infringement or not, and (2) If there is infringement, there are damages, and (3) So the damages will be a function of the infringement.

However, alignment becomes difficult with multiple patents, various patent claims, and unresolved claim-interpretation rulings throughout the litigation until shortly before or during the trial. For cases like these, you probably have to dig a little deeper to ensure alignment.

In addressing and sorting through liability and damages alignment considerations, you may decide to have your damages expert assume a certain form of damages is appropriate. For example, if you are representing a plaintiff in a patent dispute, you may ask your damages expert to prepare damages in the form of a reasonable royalty rather than go through the additional steps to establish damages in the form of lost profits. Similarly, you may choose to have your damages expert rely on a technical expert, an industry expert, or on a set of assumed facts or other witnesses.

If your damages expert is relying on other facts, assumptions, or testimony, alignment will, of course, still need to be established to support plaintiff's damages. Rather than relying on your damages expert to sort through the alignment, you will establish alignment with other witnesses or support. In such a case, you will develop the alignment between liability and the claimed damages in some manner other than through your damages expert.

Build Your Foundation on Rock

One of the great advantages of Hochosterwitz Castle, the unconquerable Austrian fortress, was its rock foundation. Rising out of the natural lines of the dolomite mountain, the castle drew strength from the solid earth underneath it.

You brought your Architect in early. You established

your Damages Sentry. You have your initial Blueprint. To establish a solid Foundation, you tested and refined your Blueprint. You defined the wrongdoing in a practical manner. You laid the groundwork to align the damages analysis to the liability case.

Now you are in a position to better anticipate and address obstacles or detours that arise as the case progresses. You are ready to dig into the damages analysis in detail. It's time for the next step in The Pragmatic Solution: the Walls.

Chapter 4

The Walls

Every day, every hour, this very minute, perhaps, dark forces attempt to penetrate this castle's walls.

— Albus Dumbledore
(*Harry Potter and the Half-Blood Prince*)

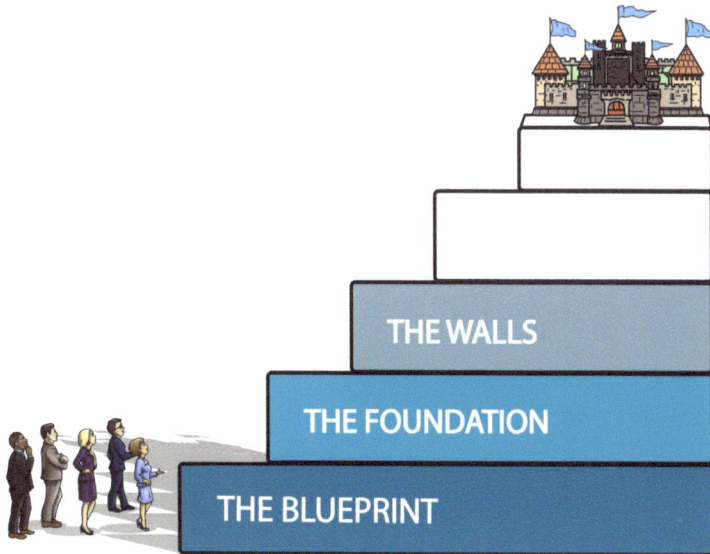

THE WALLS

THE FOUNDATION

THE BLUEPRINT

Obtain Your Building Materials

Your Blueprint provided the scope and structure to dig into the analysis. Your Damages Sentry facilitated strong communication. Your Foundation established a practical understanding of the alleged wrongdoing and alignment with liability. It is now time to start building in earnest. You will be working with your Architect to obtain the necessary and available building materials for the structure. This is the Walls phase of the Damages Castle.

Much of the damages analysis is generated during the Walls phase. The heavy lifting takes place here, and the damages analysis really kicks into high gear. In the Walls phase, your damages expert gathers the building materials for the castle from a variety of sources. The Damages Sentry often directly supplies these building materials to the damages expert.

Ask Questions

You provide your expert with relevant documents, deposition transcripts and exhibits, interrogatory questions and responses, and briefs or other legal filings. You coordinate the acquisition of additional relevant damages documents, testimony, discussions with your client, and other information.

Questions you and your expert should ask during this phase include the following: What available information is really relevant? What additional information could be relevant and attainable? Are there deposition questions that could be asked? Could there be additional document requests? Interrogatory requests? Could knowledgeable client personnel shed light on the damages analysis?

What about third-party documents or depositions? Is there relevant independent research that may be useful? Are there independent studies that could provide insights? Do you have an industry expert or technical or contract expert who could be helpful for the damages issues?

As you work through the discovery and analysis in the Walls phase, you will inevitably be adding, subtracting, and tweaking. These changes will be handled efficiently and effectively by the Damages Sentry. Throughout the construction of the Walls, you will maintain alignment between the alleged wrongdoing and the damages.

As you navigate the details of the damages analysis, you have the opportunity to work closely with your damages expert and their team. Damages-related information is obtained and analyzed throughout the discovery process. There may be extensive document and information gathering, analysis, and research.

Assumptions

The Walls may include damages assumptions. For starters, your damages expert assumes there is liability of some sort. Otherwise, no damages. Damages experts are often familiar with various forms of damages that may be available for different types of circumstances. However, damages experts are typically not legal, technical, or industry experts. You may have your damages expert base their analysis on certain assumptions. Those assumptions could be considered part of the Foundation or, alternatively, the Walls. Either way, if an assumption or assumptions are not supported or established effectively, the castle may not stand.

The Coffee Bean Filter

Granted, a coffee bean filter doesn't have anything to do with castles. It is, however, a helpful tool we have used for many years. It serves two purposes, and both contribute to building the Damages Castle. First, we use the Coffee Bean Filter as a guide and reminder to consider various potential sources of information, or building materials, for the Damages Castle.

Second, we use it as a reminder to filter the information multiple times. Reviewing documents, data, or transcripts multiple times at different stages in the damages process often proves beneficial. For example, at the beginning of the case, we are just learning the names, products, acronyms, lingo, dates, and issues. Filtering through information a second or third time later in the process, with greater understanding of the case, may reveal relevant information that was not fully recognized the first time through.

In Real Life . . . Market Share Data Confirms Industry Research

The Coffee Bean Filter can extend beyond your own review or your damages expert's review. It can also apply to your client. One such instance involved a market share analysis underlying my damages analysis in the snowplow industry. The dispute was between two competitors, and market share data was a primary variable in the analysis.

Market share data was not publicly available. The client was initially unable to identify their own independent market share data. So we performed our own extensive analysis. The analysis was solid and reasonable, but as is often the case, it was not perfect. For example, it was prepared after the historical damages period. However, the client continued to support the process. In doing so, the client uncovered internal market data that it had prepared in the normal course of business. Their market share data supported our market study. Together, they represented a solid basis for the Damages Castle.

Proactive Damages Sentry on Duty

Our firm uses the word "proactive" a lot. We use it as we discuss cases throughout the entire process. Our proactive focus grew out of our desire to reduce the number of surprises in scheduling or discovery. We have had scheduling surprises on expert report dates, deposition dates, and even trial dates. We have dealt with discovery surprises on documents and information we were not aware of.

Remember, during the Foundation phase and the beginning of the Walls phase, you likely know far more about your case than your damages expert does. You know the client personnel and many of the key documents and issues. You probably already know the terminology and acronyms. You think and dream in terms such as the "February Contract" and the "Amended Contract."

The more information you share and the more you include the expert in ongoing developments, the better they will grasp the nuances of the case. Similarly, the more you know about the expert's analysis, the better able you are to align liability and damages.

Your expert performs the bulk of the work during the Walls phase. But you, as the attorney, have the opportunity to move the damages analysis forward in an efficient, effective manner. This involves obtaining new information and identifying existing information that may be useful to the expert.

In Real Life ... Proactivity and Curiosity

I have had the pleasure of working with outstanding litigators over the years, one of whom I have worked with on a handful of cases. He asks questions. He's curious.

We communicate effectively and frequently. Through the process, we discuss and weigh potentially relevant and useful analyses. Some go forward, and some do not. As a result of that curiosity and robust communication, he has his finger on the pulse of the damages analysis as it develops.

On one occasion, we were discussing a possible additional analysis to demonstrate a particular trend. As we considered the analysis, his curiosity led us to other already available information and analyses that provided another way to demonstrate the trend. It became clear that pursuing the additional analysis was unnecessary.

He acted as a Damages Sentry by actively communicating with me. This, along with his curiosity, provided him insights into the pulse of the damages analysis.

In Real Life . . . The Proactive Damages Sentry Makes or Breaks the Walls

In the electrical-tool patent litigation with a tight timeline, the litigator provided my team and me guidance and access to information, assuring our Damages Castle was built in the proper place. He was an effective and purposeful Damages Sentry. He helped our team obtain relevant information that was difficult to get, particularly given the tight time frame. To further coordinate, he spent a few days working in our office.

Through this process of working closely with the damages expert, the Damages Sentry develops a deep understanding of your client's damages case. This is important, and it involves focusing and challenging your damages expert's analysis and opinions as they develop. It's pushing and pulling.

Perhaps your expert is unaware of certain information, and from your view, the analysis isn't shaping up as you thought it might. Maybe you don't have extensive experience working through damages analyses. So what? Don't hesitate to challenge and test the analysis or have others on your litigation team or the client challenge and test the analysis. Your damages expert can handle it. They ought to be comfortable being challenged and welcome it.

In fact, you may know important facts your expert does not know. Iron sharpens iron. This give-and-take filters out supported and unsupported variables. It builds a better castle. Without an understanding of the damages analysis, you run the risk of building a Damages Castle without sturdy walls.

Flexibility—Modular Castle Walls

Cases change directions. Certain claims, counts, patents, or parts of contracts may be eliminated from the case. For example, the trademark portion of a case may have been ruled out, but the breach of contract case remains. Different forms of damages may or may not apply to one or both or neither. Flexibility is a requirement. It's part of the litigation battle. Ideally, you build your Damages Castle with flexibility, or modular walls. If some of the walls need to be removed, will you still have a sturdy structure?

In Real Life . . . Flexibility and Shifting Liability Course

A few years ago, I was working on a patent case involving multiple patents. Both parties were asserting their own patents, meaning that both parties were essentially plaintiffs and defendants. The patents covered the same products.

As the case evolved, the court sorted through and ruled on the various issues on the different patents. The liability course shifted multiple times. Flexibility was key. The course shifted on the underlying value of the different patents. This required flexibility in developing the damages analysis for the different patents.

Test Your Architect

Throughout the Walls phase, the Damages Sentry is communicating, coordinating, and planning. As part of the process, the Damages Sentry is ideally also testing the damages analysis. Test your Architect. As the Damages Sentry, you and your litigation team likely know more about the case or the client or industry than your damages expert. The Damages Sentry is in an ideal position to test the developing analysis.

Asking questions and testing the analysis can prove useful in further developing or supporting the damages analysis and gaining a deeper understanding of the damage expert's developing analysis. Is the analysis aligning with the facts in the case? Have facts not been considered? Have additional sources of information not yet been factored into the analysis?

In Real Life . . . Double-Counting

In a breach of contract case a number of years ago in the automotive industry, the opposing side's damages analysis was vastly overstated. The opposing attorneys apparently came to realize this at trial during their expert's cross-examination. This wasn't a function of misalignment; it was a faulty calculation.

The analysis inherently double-counted a variable, undermining the calculation. Can we know this was the first time the attorneys came to realize the problem? No, we can't. Although based on their rapid exit from the courtroom at the first break during cross-examination, that sure seemed to be the case.

How did this happen? For starters, their damages analysis was not clearly presented. It was not surprising the double-counting was (apparently) missed. Did the legal team have a Damages Sentry working with the damages expert and challenging the analysis? Could proactive and consistent communication have identified and avoided the double-counting before trial?

Damages Sentry-in-Training

In some instances, our Damages Sentry has been a junior or less experienced litigator. The Damages Sentry actually offers a perfect opportunity to provide the junior attorney with effective training experience. You are matching a junior litigator with an experienced expert. My team and I have had the opportunity to be a part of many firsts with our Damages Sentries. I have been through the first deposition defended, sat in on the first deposition taken, and gone through the first trial many times with outstanding junior litigators.

Your Castle Is Nearly Complete

Not every castle needs to be on the scale of Hochosterwitz Castle on a dolomite mountain with fourteen gates. In many cases, a much smaller castle will do. Either way, you want your castle to be solid, with strong, but modular, walls. Aligning your Damages Castle to your Foundation provides the basis for strong Walls. With your damages expert, you proactively build those Walls in a purposeful manner. The Damages Sentry oversees the progress and ensures the Walls are built well. Now, it's time to create the strongest, most secure place in your castle: the Keep.

Chapter 5

The Keeps

Keep, noun: *one that keeps or protects: such as* a: *CASTLE;* specifically *the strongest and securest part of a medieval castle.*

— *Merriam-Webster*

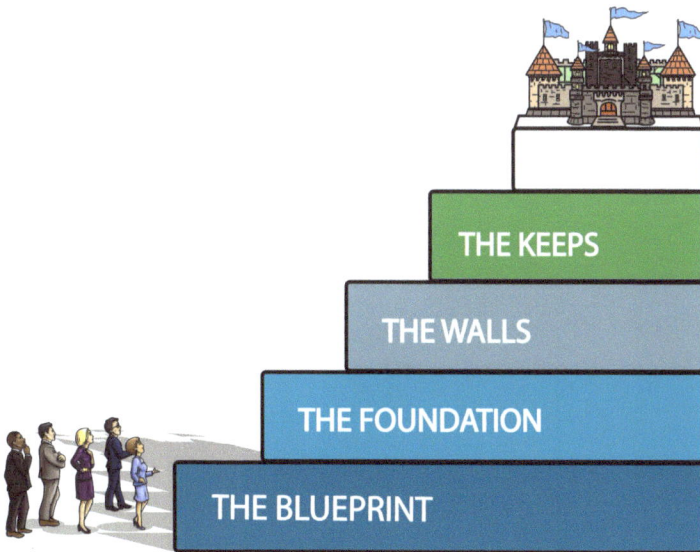

What's a Keep?

What is a Keep—and what does it have to do with your case?

Keeps are imposing, impenetrable castle towers meant to withstand even the fiercest attack. During medieval times, the keeps were used as a haven of last resort in castles under siege. Constructed of solid stone in either circular or rectangular shape, keeps could sometimes take up to a decade to build.

The Keeps in your damages case serve as your strongest defense. While they will not take you ten years to create, they do require careful construction to ensure they can adequately support your case against even the strongest attacks.

In your Damages Castle, the Keeps are key points upon which the damages analysis relies. Sometimes the Keeps are clear from the start, and other times they require analysis and digging to uncover. Either way, as your damages analysis moves forward, it's important to identify and embrace them.

The Keeps are the themes of your damages case. They may be the same as or overlap with your liability themes; or they might be different from your liability themes. At a minimum, the damages and liability themes should be aligned with each other. Your Damages Sentry assures the communication needed to achieve alignment.

The Keeps phase involves stepping back from the minutiae of the last few months of research and analysis and asking: *What really matters in this case? What is the essential information the jury should know?*

Once you have that information clear, it's just a matter of presenting it to a jury in the simplest way possible.

"Keep"-ing Your Head Up

Keeps work their way into the damages expert report and crystalize before trial. That doesn't mean you want to wait before looking for your Keeps. It's never too early to start. As in riding a mountain bike down a bumpy, twisting single-track trail, you always want to keep your head up. Starting in the Blueprint phase and working through the Foundation and the Walls, you keep your sights on identifying your Keeps. Start looking early. Keep looking. You will find them.

The Damages Expert Report

In the Walls phase, the analysis moved ahead full bore. You worked through the various analyses and handled variables, moving parts, and ongoing discovery. Now, you are heading toward your damages expert report.

The ongoing damages analysis is often detailed and full of complex financial information. It's derived from and composed of many numbers. Underlying the analysis may be relevant market information; detailed customer, manufacturing, contract, distributor, or sales capabilities; or brand information. It's easy to get twisted up and turned around in the analysis.

A damages expert report typically contains the opinions, analyses, and support upon which your expert will testify. The amount of information contained in an expert report is likely extensive. For example, the narrative portion of my reports can be one hundred pages or longer in complex cases. The schedules and analysis portion can add an additional ten to hundreds of pages to the report.

The Keeps phase filters through the details. It involves stepping back, perhaps multiple times, to identify and crystalize the most important points in the analysis. The Keeps are simple points intended to make the damages analysis clear and understandable.

This process begins during the development of the damages expert report. The report must capture the key Keeps underlying the analysis. As you are working toward the damages expert report, there may be many potential Keeps, just a few, or even just one. Some of those Keeps might overlap.

Like the keeps in a castle, your Damages Keeps put you in a place of strength and security.

Damages Sentry Maintains Post

During the development of the expert report, you or your Damages Sentry will be communicating with your damages expert. With a broader understanding and knowledge about the context of the case and ongoing developments, you ensure the damages development—and the emerging Keeps—are consistent and aligned with other parts of the case.

At the same time, you may have knowledge that circumvents or eliminates the necessity for the expert to analyze a particular area. You don't want an expert researching a particular analysis or potential Keep if there is evidence undermining it. By monitoring and communicating with your expert through the Keeps phase, you are better able to manage an efficient and effective process.

If you are the Damages Sentry, you're testing and challenging your expert's analysis. How and why is it supported? Get input from others on your litigation team and ensure your damages expert is aware of the important facts or circumstances. You will avoid falling into the blinders approach discussed in Chapter 2 and reduce the likelihood for inconsistency and misplaced Keeps.

Stepping back, slowing down, and taking inventory may help avoid a damages disaster.

Remember the medical-device patent case in the Foundation chapter, where the plaintiff's analysis was based on the successful product? The plaintiff was essentially using the product's success as a Keep. The Keep itself was great—a successful product relative to other products. However, it turned out the successful product didn't have the patented technology at issue. The Keep wasn't reinforced by the facts of the case, and their entire Damages Castle collapsed.

In Real Life . . . Keep It Simple

One complicated damages case I worked on boiled down to two words: price undercut. Converting corn to ethanol requires complex machinery and processes. The machinery and pipes get clogged with built-up material over time, requiring cleaning and maintenance. Ethanol plants periodically shut down to clean the equipment or run a large amount of sulfuric acid through the pipes.

Our client, the plaintiff, developed a process using a particular enzyme that also performed a cleaning function at a significantly lower cost than sulfuric acid. While the ethanol plants were able to save money on the enzyme process, our client was able to sell its product at a profitable premium.

The defendant was a larger supplier of components for ethanol production and had begun selling a product similar to the plaintiff's products. The defendant did so at significantly lower prices. The plaintiff lost opportunities to sell its product and faced lower competitive pricing.

Ethanol equipment, processes, and technologies are complex. Our damages analysis was detailed and data intensive. Our Keep was not. The defendant was essentially selling the same product at a lower price. Simply put, a large part of the damages centered around this price undercut. This was our primary Damages Keep. It worked because it was factual, reasonable, and simple.

The Expert Depositions

After the damages expert reports come the expert depositions. Expert depositions may happen shortly after the reports, or many months later. As a Damages Sentry who is responsible for other cases or other elements of the case at hand, your attention will likely turn away from damages during this lull; the same applies to your damages expert.

During this period, there may be ongoing discovery, additional depositions, document production, interrogatory responses, or court rulings. The opposing damages expert's report may be submitted along with other relevant experts' reports, such as those from industry or technical experts.

If the break is long, there could be months or even years of additional financial or market information that are relevant to damages. The time away and the introduction of these new variables might help clarify the case. Alternatively, this information could make things more complicated.

Working toward the expert's deposition provides the opportunity to refocus on your damages expert, their analysis, and the Keeps. You communicate with your expert before the deposition and in preparation for the opposing damages expert's deposition. This communication may help crystalize your understanding of and focus on the Damages Keeps.

Working Toward Your Trial

The Walls are up, your Keeps have been constructed, and your damages expert deposition is complete. What's next? Perhaps it's the deposition of the opposing damages expert or ongoing discovery. Maybe all you have to do is hold tight until damages-related motions or briefs are due before trial. As your case marches toward trial, you have peace of mind knowing your Castle is built with strong Keeps.

In the next chapter, we will look at going to trial with your Damages Castle. While much of the heavy lifting of castle construction is behind you, this is not the time to put damages aside. Strong focus and coordination at this stage ensures that you use the Damages Castle to your best advantage.

Chapter 6

The Castle

A field of clay touched by the genius of man becomes a castle.

— Og Mandino

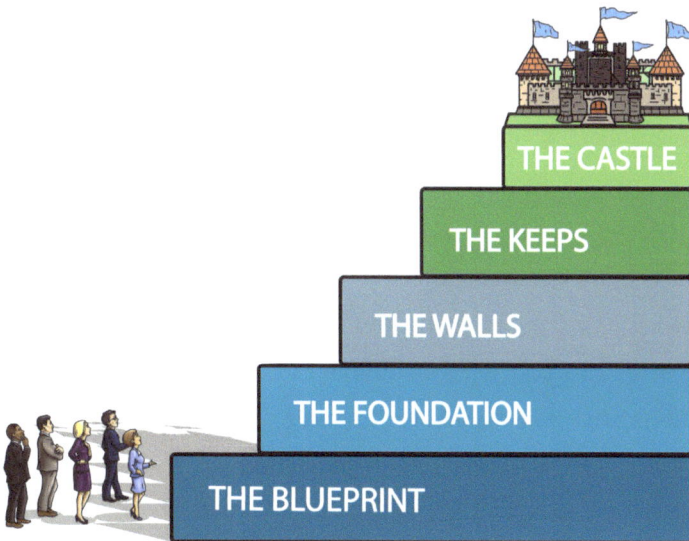

The Damages Sentry Under Pressure

Now it's time to prepare for trial. The pace quickens, and you are often pulled in many directions.

As you and your team gear up, will you be able to keep your focus on your damages case? Will the trier of fact understand and appreciate your Damages Castle? In this chapter, we will discuss trial preparation and presentation and getting the trier of fact into your Castle. After all, you have worked so hard on it, you want them to appreciate your Castle. Hopefully, it's as strong as the Hochosterwitz.

Keep Your Damages Sentry on Guard

As you prepare for trial, everything ramps up and expands exponentially, including nonstop motions and corresponding unresolved issues.

Does it make sense to involve your damages expert and their team to address some of these motions and related issues? Are you planning to file a *Daubert* motion? Respond to one? Do you need to prepare any motions in limine? At this point, you are likely juggling many different responsibilities. It may seem like a good time to cut the Damages Sentry. We see this happen—a lot.

We are not lawyers, but we have seen and worked through many of these issues in our cases. Continual communication with your expert is always beneficial. Talking through these issues with your expert will naturally align your mutual understanding of potential limitations, exposures, adjustments, or updates as you are working toward trial.

In Real Life . . . When the Damages Sentry Is Removed

A few years ago, we were looking toward an upcoming patent trial. Our client was the defendant. There had been a short lull in communication since my deposition. That's to be expected. Up until my deposition, there had been various attorneys who somewhat collectively had taken on the Damages Sentry role. The trial was scheduled in a few weeks.

I was out of the country the week before trial, returning the day before the trial was to begin. We wanted to be prepared, so before I left for my trip, my colleague and I scheduled a conference call with the litigation team members, primarily to discuss my direct testimony and the cross-examination of the plaintiff's damages expert.

During the short call, the attorneys told us they would prepare my testimony and the cross of the plaintiff's expert. They asked us not to prepare my direct testimony, identify trial exhibits, or prepare any demonstrative exhibits. We were also told not to prepare cross-examination topics or questions for the opposing damages expert. They essentially wanted us to sit tight until further notice.

Fast forward to the trial. The case was bifurcated. We received a call after the jury returned with a willful infringement verdict. As the defendant's damages expert, my testimony would be last. There were numerous witnesses for both parties, meaning there were multiple witnesses and cross-examinations to prepare. One of those cross-examinations was for the plaintiff's damages expert. The litigators had not prepared for that cross-examination. They also had not prepared for my testimony.

Fortunately, after that phone conference weeks before, my colleague and I had recognized it was our responsibility, regardless, to prepare for the trial.

Now, in the midst of the trial and with the liability verdict in, the lead litigator asked me whether we had any thoughts for cross-examination of the plaintiff's damages expert. We had prepared for the cross-examination, but we had done so in a vacuum. We had no guidance on the issues leading up to and during trial, nor had we been at the liability portion of the trial. We had not prepared with a Damages Sentry.

In the end, the jury came back with a damages verdict closer to our number than the plaintiff's number. From a pure damages standpoint, it sounds like a win for the defendant, given the willful infringement ruling.

Maybe.

But we wonder what would have happened with a dedicated Damages Sentry throughout the case and trial.

Bridging the Gap

Ultimately, a trial is about telling your client's story to the trier of fact. At this point, you're overflowing with case-specific knowledge. Your challenge is to communicate your client's story to people who don't have all of your knowledge. Todd Goldberg of NorthStar Lit Technologies calls this "bridging the gap." Todd has consulted and participated in more than two hundred trials, arbitrations, and mediations. He has seen this challenge many times.

Part of bridging the gap is being able to show off your Damages Castle with its strong Walls, solid Foundation, and formidable Keeps. As sturdy as your Damages Castle is, it also has a deep moat around it, making it difficult to communicate with the outside world. You know how and why your Damages Castle is strong. Can those outside your castle appreciate its strength?

Your moat is overflowing with industry and company terminology, market data, financial and accounting jargon, acronyms, and financial spreadsheets. You've been immersed in this terminology for months or possibly years. The jurors have not.

How do you create a clear damages picture? You may want to test your ability to bridge the gap before charging straight into trial. A mock trial may provide you with the ideal format to test your story. Fellow attorneys not involved in your case may offer another option. What about testing your story on family members or friends (albeit recognizing potential confidentiality constraints)?

Alignment with the liability case is the first underlying step. You've already addressed that in your Foundation stage. The Damages Sentry's communication and coordination with your Architect will similarly promote your ability to bridge the gap.

Your Keeps will then guide your damages story. Remember the complicated ethanol case? Price undercut clarified the complex damages analysis. It bridged the gap.

In Real Life . . . Show-and-Tell—A Suitcase and a Canoe

Some cases may offer additional opportunities to bridge the gap. In a suitcase patent trial a number of years ago, we used a show-and-tell to bridge the gap. After the plaintiff presented their claimed royalty damages, we showed the jurors the suitcases. We pointed out where the accused technology was in the suitcases. A simple show-and-tell. It bridged the gap.

In another patent trial, we used a similar approach. This case involved a certain type of canoe. We showed the jurors the canoes with the patented technology. While the trial did not make it to completion, it appeared the gap had been bridged, judging by the jurors' nodding heads.

In Real Life . . . Widening the Gap

A damages testimony not supported by the rest of the case may fail to bridge the gap. Remember the case where the jurors had not heard about the defendant's low sales and profits prior to my testimony? Those low sales and profits framed the plaintiff's claimed damages as being far in excess of the defendant's sales and profits. Yet the defendant's witnesses had not talked about them. After listening to many witnesses, the first time the jurors heard about the defendants' low sales and profits was during my testimony. Presenting these low figures for the first time so late in the trial did not help bridge the gap. Perhaps, this even widened the gap.

Damages Sentry Handoffs

Cases ebb and flow, and priorities, responsibilities, and workloads shift. Often, the Damages Sentry becomes a tag team of two or more litigators. In some ways, this provides flexibility as the case progresses. With the Damages Sentry approach, tag teams and handoffs can work well.

Back in Chapter 2, I introduced the concept of the handoff. Often the handoff involves a less-experienced litigator handing off the Damages Sentry role to a more experienced litigator. This type of handoff is quite common. In some instances, it is a more-experienced Damages Sentry handing off to a less experienced Damages Sentry.

Handoffs can be quite effective. But there are also risks.

In Real Life . . . A Bobbled Handoff

Sometimes handoffs are not executed with proper foresight. One such case involved a senior litigator who acted as one of multiple Damages Sentries during the damages case. He generally knew my analysis and the damages issues. As trial approached, he was juggling various witnesses and responsibilities, as were the other Damages Sentries with knowledge of the damages issues. A Damages Sentry void developed.

A handoff took place the evening prior to my testimony. The new Damages Sentry had limited litigation experience and was unfamiliar with the damages issues. The new Damages Sentry was not going to be taking my direct testimony, but rather was working through my testimony with me in preparation for the more senior litigator to ask the relevant questions during my testimony. It was a tough spot for the new Damages Sentry.

The relevant testimony did come through. But the testimony could have been smoother. It could have been clearer. Did it ultimately matter? Of course, we don't know. What we do know is that a better-planned Damages Sentry handoff to the junior litigator in the weeks leading up to trial would have been useful for the litigator, the testimony process, and the testimony itself.

In Real Life . . . A Well-Executed Handoff

One particular case provides insight into an effective handoff. On a contract case in the window industry, our team was brought in early. Communication was clear, focused, and comprehensive. As usual, there were lulls in the case from a damages standpoint. Nonetheless, updates and communication continued.

The lead litigator worked closely with us throughout much of the damages analysis and deposition. He was the initial Damages Sentry. Then he handed off Damages Sentry duties to another litigator as the case shifted beyond the damages report and deposition toward trial. Importantly, this shift took place well in advance of trial. It was an effective handoff because the new Damages Sentry had been intimately involved in the overall case throughout and was familiar with the damages analysis.

As we turned our attention toward trial, the roles were clear. Communication flowed between the Damages Sentries, us, and the other litigators on their team. The Damages Sentries prepared witnesses and prepared for cross-examinations, and we created trial exhibits and demonstrative evidence. The liability and damages cases were aligned.

It was time for direct damages testimony. The lead litigator watched as his co-counsel walked through the questions. After his co-counsel sat down, he whispered, "That was the best damages direct I have seen."

Why? They used a Damages Sentry throughout the case, and the handoff was effective.

Is Your Support in Place?

Here are some basic questions you may consider as you prepare for the damages portion of trial:

- What evidence do you need for your damages case?
- Who will testify to and support that evidence?
- What testimony do you want from your own witnesses?
- Is your damages expert relying on certain facts provided primarily by testimony?
- Who are the best people to testify to those facts?
- How much time will be needed for each witness?
- Do you have an industry expert or a technical expert testifying on damages issues?
- Who on your team is handling each of these witnesses?
- What deposition testimony aligns with and supports your damages expert's testimony and analysis?

A picture speaks a thousand words. Is your damages expert preparing demonstratives? Providing input on their exhibits is an opportunity to align the damages case with the liability case.

What about the opposing side's case? Who is cross-examining the opposing side's witnesses? Is the cross-examining attorney on your team sufficiently prepared on the relevant damages topics? What trial exhibits will you use in cross-examination?

Opening Statements and Your Keeps

Who will do the opening statement? How will damages be addressed in the opening statement? If the trial is bifurcated, has there been preparation in advance of the trial? Is the litigator most knowledgeable on the damages issues doing the opening statement? If it's a team member who is less familiar with the damages analysis and Keeps, you run the risk of confusing, overstating, or understating what the jurors will hear.

As you approach the opening statements—whether in a bifurcated or non-bifurcated trial—use them as an opportunity to align your liability and damages stories for the trier of fact. This is your first chance to lay the initial groundwork for key damages testimony and exhibits.

Cross-Examining the Opposing Expert and Your Keeps

Let's assume your client is the defendant. You're on deck to cross the opposing expert, and your damages expert hasn't testified yet. Hopefully you have been working through the damages issues leading up to this point with your own damages expert. You have sorted and filtered through the Keeps in your expert's analysis. You have unwound and understood the plaintiff's damages analysis. If so, you're well prepared to develop and then cross the opposing expert.

You will be in a position to focus on what really matters: the points that are consistent with your expert's analysis and the key challenges to the opposing side's analysis.

When you are working with the defendant, preparing the cross-examination of the opposing expert provides another opportunity to align your liability arguments with your damages expert's analysis before they testify.

Cross-examination is also a great time to reinforce your Keeps. In one trial, after a cross-examination that touched on many relatively minor points, our litigator directly circled back to our main Keep: damages were really about one particular customer. He had worked closely with us through the entire damages process. He knew the analysis, the document and testimony support, the damages context, and the key points. In other words, he was an active Damages Sentry and laser focused on the main Keep.

Let's consider the alternative scenario wherein you have not involved your own damages expert in your trial preparation. Perhaps you took the opposing expert's deposition a few months ago, and you don't think you need to rely on any input from your own damages expert. Do you know your Keeps? Are you sure? Are you assuming your expert is doing whatever they are supposed to be doing while preparing to testify? What if they are unprepared? What if they aren't prepared to communicate effectively and succinctly? What are their Damages Keeps?

The Pragmatic Solution in Practice

Every case is different. The clients, issues, timing, risks, damages amounts, and resources available vary in every case. Through all of these differences, The Pragmatic Solution and the steps outlined in this book can generally apply to your damages cases.

In Real Life . . . The Pragmatic Solution from Start to Finish

A patent trial I testified at several years ago offers a positive example of The Pragmatic Solution in action.

The Blueprint: The attorneys in that case consulted with our team from the early stages of the case. The client was the plaintiff. The litigator team established a Damages Sentry. She was an experienced litigator and also experienced in working with a damages expert. We worked together initially mapping out potential damages approaches.

The Foundation: We initially worked through the process of developing a practical understanding of the patented technology. The Damages Sentry coordinated the process and communication between the legal team, the technical expert, the inventor, and others.

The Walls: The Damages Sentry did an outstanding job keeping us updated on case developments, including discovery issues, motions filed, and other issues. She coordinated and informed her litigation team members on the damages issues and developments. She helped coordinate our access to the necessary building materials for the Damages Castle. She and others on the litigation team approached the analysis with a healthy skepticism. In doing so, the team built an understanding and confidence in the analysis.

The Keeps: Through the process it became clear there were several damages themes. They were all built into my expert report.

My deposition took place relatively soon after my expert report. Then, from a damages standpoint, the case went dormant for some time as liability rulings and appeals sorted themselves out. During this time, the Damages Sentry periodically kept us apprised of developments.

The Castle: As the case regained steam and began heading toward trial, we dusted off the old files, re-immersed ourselves in the case facts, and got rolling again. The Damages Sentry set aside a day, weeks before trial, to walk through my direct testimony, including trial exhibits and demonstrative exhibits.

We spent that day with another litigation teammate and one of my colleagues. One of the damages themes shone through. It clearly aligned with both the liability and damages cases—the strongest Keep.

As is so often the case during a hectic trial, our Damages Sentry ended up being pulled in multiple directions. When I sat down to testify, it was just after lunch. She began, "Good morning, Mr. Bero." I noted it was actually afternoon. She looked at me, laughed, and dove into her questions.

While she momentarily lost track of the time of day, she knew our analysis, our Keeps, and the other side's analysis inside and out. The client ended up with a significant damages award.

Preparing for Post-Trial

We know that cases often don't end with the trial; they go on to appeal. Or maybe the case doesn't make it to trial before appeal, or just part of the case makes it to trial the first time. Regardless, trial is the primary opportunity to submit your damages evidence for post-trial motions, appeals, or related or subsequent trials.

When you arrive at the damages phase at trial, you're likely near the end of testimony. Everyone involved is tired. You could be tempted to rush through the damages as quickly as possible so everyone can just get on with it. You don't want the damages expert or other damages witnesses to bore the jurors or upset the judge for taking too much time.

At the same time, you have to be sure you're providing enough information and foundation to prepare for the post-trial motions and appeals. Resist the urge to rush through damages. What you submit into evidence at trial could pay off for you months or years down the road as the case evolves.

In Real Life . . . Multiple Trials

We had one case in which multiple patents were asserted. Our client was the plaintiff, and our analysis showed that one of the asserted patents was truly valuable; the others were less so. We based our Keeps on this premise, and I testified to it in my deposition.

Just before trial, the judge issued a claim construction opinion on the valuable patent, leading to a summary judgment ruling of noninfringement on that patent. The trial went forward on the less valuable patents. Our side never wavered. We stuck to our Keeps, one of which was the idea that the one patent excluded from trial was the most valuable technology. The other side's expert was happy to agree with us.

We presented a damages range for the less valuable patents. Our analysis was accurate, fair, and pragmatic, and our client was awarded damages toward the higher end of the damages range.

Fast forward a few years. The valuable patent ruling was reversed on appeal and the parties were again headed toward trial. The valuable patent Keep from the first trial boomeranged back into play. The opposing expert struggled to explain his prior testimony on this valuable patent. The jury awarded significantly higher damages than the first trial, closely approximating the amount we presented.

Go Build a Castle

The Pragmatic Solution isn't complicated, but it is a commitment. It's a commitment to walk through these steps with your team and your damages expert.

If you or your firm would like to speak with me or my team about a damages case, please feel free to contact me at rbero@berogroup.com. You can learn more about our firm at www.berogroup.com.

Navigating commercial litigation cases is not easy. You know that. You also know damages is one of the pieces of your commercial litigation puzzle. It can often be an important piece. The Pragmatic Solution will help you through.

By employing The Pragmatic Solution, you are tapping into the experience of your damages expert to create a well-reasoned and fully supported damages case that aligns with your liability case.

Building a castle can seem daunting. But if done with a

skilled team and a solid plan, it will come together. Stone by stone, tower by tower, you end up building an impressive and powerful structure.

I hope this book will help you and your team build a Damages Castle that stands strong on the litigation battlefield.

ABOUT THE AUTHOR

Over the last thirty plus years, Rick Bero has built a career as a pragmatic damages expert with a deep financial background and broad litigation experience. He has testified at approximately 40 trials. In total, he has testified as an expert more than 150 times in federal and state courts, depositions, arbitrations, and other hearings across the United States.

A certified public accountant (CPA) and a certified valuation analyst (CVA), Rick is the founder and managing director of The BERO Group. He and his team provide accounting and financial consulting services and expert testimony pertaining to economic damages and valuation issues in a wide range of litigation matters with an emphasis on commercial litigation, intellectual property and fraud / forensic investigations.

Rick's commercial litigation experience includes breach

of contract, anti-trust, tortious interference, fraud, false advertising, dealership disputes, and lender liability. His intellectual property litigation and valuation experience includes utility and design patents, trademarks, copyrights, trade dress, and trade secrets.

Rick has served as an expert in intellectual property litigations covering a wide range of technologies, including manufacturing, electronics, medical imaging, medical devices, software, construction and heavy equipment, automotive, consumer products, and many others.

The BERO Group was formerly part of Corporate Financial Advisors, LLC, a firm Rick co-founded in 1995. Prior to that, Rick was the Wisconsin practice leader for Coopers & Lybrand's National Litigation & Claims Service practice and an executive consultant with Peterson Consulting in Chicago and Milwaukee.

Rick has presented, provided instruction, and written articles on topics like intangible assets, intellectual property damages, working with experts, and accounting issues. Rick authored the chapters on patent infringement damages and trade secret damages in *The Comprehensive Guide to Economic Damages*, currently in its fifth edition. He has been the lead instructor of the intellectual property damages course for the National Association of Certified Valuation Analysts and is a former instructor for an international CPA review course.

Over the years, my team and I have developed *The Pragmatic Solution* while working on many different damages cases with numerous law firms and attorneys. We believe *The Pragmatic Solution* is an effective way to approach economic damages, from the perspective of both damages experts and attorneys. I am excited to share *The Pragmatic Solution* in my book: *The Litigator's Damages Blueprint: The Pragmatic Solution*. My hope is this process will help litigators build a strong damages analysis.

For further information about The BERO Group, please call us at 262.522.7920, visit us online at www.berogroup. com, or email us at info@berogroup.com. Also see us at https://www.linkedin.com/company/the-bero-group.

www.ingramcontent.com/pod-product-compliance
Lightning Source LLC
Chambersburg PA
CBHW041118210326
41518CB00031B/151